BACK TO FORTH

BACK TO FORTH
Gloria Frym

The Figures

Cover art: detail from *Ladder III*, 1979 by Bella Tabak Feldman

Special thanks to J.E. Jouris and Summer Brenner

Copyright © 1982 by Gloria Frym

Earlier versions of some of these works were published
in: *Soup, Rejection, Pequod, Center, Periodics, Pacific
Poetry & Fiction Review, San Marcos View, Cross Country,
Networks:* An Anthology of San Francisco Bay Area Women's
Poetry (Vortex Editions, 1979)

Publication of this book was partially supported by a
grant from the National Endowment for the Arts.
Published by The Figures, 2016 Cedar, Berkeley, California 94709.

Distributed by *Small Press Distribution, Inc.,* 1784 Shattuck Ave.,
Berkeley, CA 94709; *Bookslinger,* 330 E. 9th St., Saint Paul,
MN 55101; *Barbary Coast,* 635 Amador St., Richmond, CA 94805;
Segue, 300 Bowery, New York, N.Y. 10012; *New York State Small
Press Association,* P.O. Box 1264, Radio City Station, New York,
NY 10101

ISBN 0-935724-09-5

Table of Contents

IV. REFLEXIVE

It lies ahead, a horizon, a semicircle; but the ends of this semi-circle are joined by a sinew, and the plane of this sinew goes right through the middle of the world.

—Robert Musil

I. Charms of a Beheld Landscape

He Complains "She Won't Talk
Dirty to Me Anymore"

All of your problems have to do with words. Which one to use, how many to get there, why to use them, who to give them to, when to discard them, where to put them. You may take tea with a stranger between 4 and 6, you may easily take one day at a time, if you were once inclined to abuse days, but you really cannot take words that way. All words have a hidden future. At dusk you may write the word *tree* and it grows leaves from the shadows and the leaves fall to meet their own reflections, and so on. The word *promise* can tender long term conspiracies. From the comfort of your wicker chair on the veranda, with a tooth-pick in your teeth, you may listen to the space between words and no-words. But underneath the skin of silence, the custard of words bubbles. Sometimes in the presence of another person, you will notice an airless absence of speech between you. You feel a choke and smoke begins to curl from the combustion of words rubbing against each other inside your chest. And there is much danger in protecting yourself with too many words. Nature repeats herself but words grow poorly in the wild. Young girls often defend themselves from words by giggling or applying lipstick to their mouths. Words leaving the room without permission sometimes lose their meaning, though often the injection of one word, such as *yes* during intercourse, is worth a hundred actions.

The Little World Unto Yourself

You wake up. You think about your dream. You watch the finches at the feeder. You drink your coffee. You write down your thought about the finches at the feeder. You make your list. You sit down to do one of the items on your list. The phone rings, it is for you, it is some woman calling from the Red Victorian Hotel telling you how much she likes your book. You find a blanket, you lay it out on your patio in the sun and you take off your shirt. Your breasts are full. Your neighbors are spit shining their car; you wonder if they notice you half naked in the sun. You think a thought about the safety of living next to men who love men; you both like and dislike your exemption. You think a thought about your mother. Within the thought is your recent decision to send her things you like. You wonder what your ex-husband is doing this time of day, though what brought you to this thought was a previous thought about the balminess of the afternoon and your memory of lying beneath him on the grass, in your old backyard, after planting the sweet-peas. Before that, you thought about the garden and how you would arrange it and why you weren't doing it just now. You try to finish the first task on your list but you do not. You think another thought about yourself, about the imperfection of your skin. You have a thought about taking one of your coats to the cleaners. You think another thought about a certain man, the thought is not about him but about how you can surprise him. When he calls later, you are concerned about the quality of your voice, whether the anxiety of the day will show through. You think about the visual safety of telephones, how you are nervous and how your voice might betray you. You are aware of gesturing with your hands while you are talking on the phone. You talk a lot and keep him on the line longer than he wants. The phone rings again and you do the same thing with the next person. You hang up and think about how you need to keep talking. You feed yourself, you remark on the quality of your ravenousness. You have a thought that you are aware of avoiding yourself all day. You think about this while you are avoiding thinking about how to stop avoiding yourself. You have a thought about how your thoughts are all over the place, how you should go inside. You write a postcard you can send out of yourself, it begins with *I*. You think about the trees growing full. You remember every year you have thought about them before now. Each year has a different color in your thoughts, one in particular is a convulsive impasto. Then all the years separate into fractured hues. You have a thought about how you were always at the center of all your loves, except perhaps your love of certain flowers or small birds. Even those remind you of yourself, as though you were a landscape and they were in you.

At a party, all the guests were orphans. One expressed that she didn't like body contact. She spoke rarely but when she did, she would turn her body from the conversation slightly and always tell a story that included a list, at the end of which she would trail off with the phrase, "and so on."

Another of the guests recently inherited a house. He seemed grateful that no money was involved and spoke highly of the neighborhood. His grandmother birthed nineteen children and outlived all but four. At twenty he had a vasectomy, not wanting, he said, to be a slave to his body.

A third guest said he used to fast for fifteen days taking only grape juice. Also he would run twenty miles a day. He liked, he said, the idea of his stomach touching his spine, he wanted his body to be as perfect as an idea. His wife was rather plump.

A fourth guest described a Japanese movie about blind orphan girls who went about the countryside singing for rice at the doorsteps of strangers. One orphan was expelled from her group for attracting a handsome man, though her sense of him was only that he could see.

Orphans look like anybody else in the moonlight though they might not think so. One thought she was invisible unless the phone rang, or a letter came from someone she barely knew or there was someone in the house when she came home from work. Another claimed he was his own parents, which decreased an outsider's chance for entering such a tight knit family.

Whatever you give some orphans they will assume it is love. Partial orphans, that is those with invisible fathers, respond in a similar fashion. The one across the street thinks everything is food. Her house is surrounded by edible plants, her chickens are named Chocolate, Strawberry, Vanilla, etc., and her dog is named Biscuit or Crumb.

The man who gave the party fell in love with an orphan. He sent her small presents, he clipped articles for her on subjects that might interest her, he invited her to dinner quite often. When at last he spoke of marriage, she asked to meet his family. Afterwards, the couple began to argue over small things. Finally the orphan revealed that she could not marry a man who had such perfect parents.

Good Morning

He could leap out of bed called by an alarm only he could hear. He could saunter into the shower. He could shut the shower door and rattle the tiny wired hexagons of glass. I could see him in silhouette, soaping down his private places. He could step out of the shower and rub his shoulders with the white towel. He could stand in front of the steamy mirror brushing his teeth, with the towel draped around his waist. He could comb his hair but leave it wet and slicked back, the moisture gravitating down to the ends, a few drops stuck to his cheeks below his sideburns. He could sashay into the kitchen and put the kettle on to boil. He could call out, "coffee," in a throaty voice. I could moan back, "uh-huh." He could return to the bedroom and stand in front of the open closet. The towel could slip from his hips. He could bend over to pick it up and throw it on the bed. I could feel the weight of the towel land on my ankles. His straight hair could curl slightly behind his right ear. I could follow the curl down the side of his neck around to the ten or fifteen strands of russet fuzz on his chest. He could have a faint vertical line of down running from his chest to his lower stomach, branching into his red pubic mound. The red telephone could ring and he could stand by the bed with his right hand on his white hip just below his tan line. He could slowly sit down on the bed and even more languorously lay his head on the pillow as he continued to speak into the phone. I could lean over and kiss his left shoulder which could smell like English lavender. I could bend my head down and kiss his tightening thigh. I could let my tongue move all the way down his thigh to his ankle. I could grab both his ankles and spread his firm legs apart. I could hear his voice quiver into the phone. I could crawl in between his legs, I could nest my head between his thighs, I could make him late for work.

Charms of a Beheld Landscape

A half remembered thought lives only part of its life in the open. Mostly the sweet instrument hangs in the corner and plays to itself. Your current ear completes the music.

This paper surrenders to the type. Each letter, a stroke of dark on white. Your eye on the filled page releases a new light.

You leave a glance. It is the dropped handkerchief of ambivalent desire. Someone else returns the meaning.

From a vertical stance, what can be said about the sky is too big to say. Blue is dense in the passive voice. From a parallel position, you may frame the sky through the thick vines of the passion flower. Platoons of clouds march by in their aggressive silence.

The landscape completes itself.

You Will Be Identified by the Company You Keep

I am frequently alone and my friends are loners. Since nature abhors a vacuum, no desire goes unfilled. You believe a certain kindness will protect you. In order to get me to leave sooner, the waitress ignored my empty coffee cup. Sounds take revenge, the dog barks from abandonment. If we let you sit in a booth alone, we'll have to make exceptions for all the singles. Upon rising, he whistled a few bars of, *"my romance doesn't need a thing but you."* The world is made of more parties of two than four. They did not appreciate my writing in public, it reminded them of work. After the cough was over, the cougher appeared happier. Where the thought leads, many sizes fit none. Some acts resemble the wrong letter in the right envelope. You would like to be free of this, her painted nails remind you of all you said no to. She said, be a good girl, thank your soul for returning to you each morning. I will go for broke, I will advertise for the lost music. The shelves wait, the bookjacket is still too big for the book. She did not come to audit, she was only looking for the place where the light divides.

Spectator Sport

From the bottom of the stairs, the cat watched the squirrel in the tree and she watched both of them from behind the window. She also tried to watch herself watch them. But each time she turned to the mirror on the wall next to the window, she could no longer watch herself watching the animals. For a moment, as she was watching the cat watch the squirrel, she thought she would imagine that someone was watching her so she would watch harder. She decided a certain man was watching her. That day, he asked her if he could watch her masturbating. He said that watching her give herself pleasure gave him more pleasure than giving her pleasure. After ten minutes of watching her from behind, he already knew she used to dance. He expressed, however, no interest, when she suggested a night at the ballet. In the morning, she enjoyed him watching her watch two Jehovah's Witnesses walk down the block with copies of *The Watchtower* under their arms. By the afternoon, during a ballgame on *TV*, she didn't really enjoy him watching her watch the fans in the grandstand. She noticed him blink as she watched a small part of a camera move across the screen. By that night she became paranoid because a strange man seemed to know too much when she first met him. She wondered how long he had been watching her before she imagined he was watching her. It wasn't long before she installed tiny side view mirrors on her glasses in order to watch him watch her every move. Soon she saw him watching every person he encountered as if each were guilty of all the crimes she had committed.

Blush

In those days, the lost pilot imagined highways below. Signals often gave off signals of their own or roamed the lonely stratosphere unreceived. The signals wanted, as all things want, to take a hostage, if only for the night, if only for some unnamed bliss to answer. It was almost Halloween and the abyss filled a type of tenderness. Snow arrived suddenly from the East and I had pressed the apples as far as they would go. And there lay the chestnuts in their spiny pods. I was ready for the marron glacé. It was all by previous engagement. So what was our complaint? Only that the trees had no use for us. And we were in love with the leaves. What were we to do with such long distance operations? One desires, one does not desire, and in between a vague meadow of halves. There was no avoiding melancholy joy, wondering whether this would be the last one of many or the first of several more. We saw the perfect space between snow geese in flight. The disembodied color reached us.

II. Diminishing Return

Put Another Fake Log on the Fire
in the Beautiful False Thicket

This the pretend one. This quick dip into the future sky and
the blue stain on our lips. False blue! Paper lips! This the
occasional pair of training wheels until. Could it be that false
and less confuse themselves in this our limitless world? Visible
with the usual tricks of visibility. One island universe struck
through the heart of another island universe and passed on into
space again. The same hot illusion every time! A finger in the
silence points back into the silence pretending to be brave. The
training is vigorous. Like waiting for afterlife. Observe the
obvious signs of forgery: the alligator gods of your history
aren't still biting your thigh and this is not a real summer night.

Back to Forth

We were misdirected by native guides. I was burning into the dark index. At that time all light hurt my eyes, but I traced you to where you might have been, sleeping the night off, playing a sort of lyric born of discontent. We compared notes, a chill fluttered across our sleeveless shoulders, our soft arm hair blew and lay down again against its rightful skin, we leaned against the organ cactus and we posed. Are the snapshots ready? Are you ready? Or shall we go for a ride in the bumper cars. Will the rally always be like this, the odds fixed, the ceaseless double clutch, the battering of tender fenders. And you know you cannot hurt yourself, you are protected by circumspection, except for the chance of a runaway buggy, a deep breath, an unexpected phone call, a spark from off the track. I'll bet on it. Do you suppose these fires start alone? You blew on them. And now the copter hovers above the scene, the bodies banished, the sirens approach the building. Some darlings cuddle some island poses as a kingsize bed, some teenagers arriving in ankle bracelets temporarily restore the percale to the sheets. Some feet shuffle, some blushes appear on the cheeks of the tired, you can't remember what you ate but you still believe the drink was poisoned by the opposition. They didn't say it would be like this, throwing messages into the water without bottles, the long pier that drops off and then begins again suddenly, the gulls, the perch, the live and edible bait. Meanwhile, the sun makes certain demands, silver linings, happiness which was always the issue but never the point. Years later and you are still eavesdropping, the tar on the roof as soft as the day it was poured.

Mist Net

On the pier. Which drops off suddenly, then resumes. On the loose. Knot that pulls all the threads together. Walking up the stairs in the dark. The memory of one foot following the other. The cart forever bearing the horse. Dogs barking long before the sirens whine. Call in the cats: here Mommy, here Geezer, here Fatboy. If me, then. First, the fingerprint under the magnifier. Then telephone all correspondents to insure receipt of new voiceprint. Then order two pieces of toast, hold the bread please. Migration. Plenty happening, where to locate it. Station to station. Clock that never stops, bath oil no bathtub, and the embassy lies in ruin. All your clothes draped over the backs of rocking chairs in the bedroom, living room, anteroom, driveway. The territory of anything goes invaded by nothing doing. Now you know, now you don't! Migration. Navigation. Where you are is not a spot. When *your* beep beep goes off, *my* beep beep. Why are you a grownup? At sunset, all the gulls rise up from the beach and fly off into the darkening sea.

Gnaw

An alarm clock is ringing in your esophagus. Hunger: the body always objected, now it revolts. So afraid of hunger, so loyal to your own ideas, you won't give them up. There you are, grinning like a toothless prizefighter in front of the open refrigerator. You quickly stuff all the raw meat into your pockets. An animal blinded by the light moves toward, rather than away from, the oncoming vehicle. The ping of the bulb blowing out, then the hot current with nowhere to go. Hunger: the loss of touch. Mothers and fathers, please trim your fingernails and remove your diamond rings before feeding baby. These problems are a function of one another. You think you've solved one when another swaggers into the room, drunk on milk and wailing in its own set of wet diapers. You are so hungry by now that you trip on the cord that connects you to the light. The loss of touch. You could talk to the one who looks well-fed, but he is hungry too. And if you sit very still, you can hear four people typing in the same house.

Faithful to the Text

Take a pitchfork to the fallen petals. What falls. Raining, we consider the number of stars that cannot be seen. Yearn for what we know is. Lust, a simple rise. The mind overprocessing the gesture. Did he mean. As I write the word *remarkable,* my mind remarks her numerous qualities. Movement, negotiate each step. A line of least resistance. Who surrenders.

I didn't know you were so good, I didn't dream you could. We were introduced five times. I could never forget your crewcut. The overgrown lawn. The wicker chair I sat you in as I unzipped your pegged pants.

Implied promise. The rules. How he hates the words *I know* and *never.* The ensuing anarchy. Desire. The south of France. The slopes he skied down. The curve of their spines on the feather bed. Whose definition matters. What sinks in soft.

Running we consider what rises. Steam is how we speak. The room evaporates. The walls, down to the brick. The feathers of the bird perched in the branches. The bones flown away.

Diminishing Return

It worked once so I try it again. It didn't work so I try it again. Like a train on a track controlled by a box held by a little person at XMAS. Never really tired of the same curves. Inability to cross off anyone in my address book even after they've died. My plan is hard to get but I'm not. I could set out thirty things on my doorstep and she'd still want something that wasn't there. I wish I had a roll top head, I wish I had a clue. I stick with her because she's a test. Sounds like a hippo afraid of an alligator. But it's my fate, the patio encircled by cactus, rose bushes and no path. Every day I brush against the same spines and spend hours pulling the small hairs on my own arms. I don't know about Them anymore after so many years of suspecting. I am a little bored I make a little trouble, then I sweep it up. Word like a match. Thanks, I'll light my own today. Normally it doesn't matter, but if I don't answer the ringing phone, the front door slams, the fuse blows, the toilet overflows. A woodpecker lifts a stray elm twig from the sidewalk and flies away. The big ideas are about such small things. People can die from their own dreams. "If you ran into an old boyfriend, would the years look better on him than you?" I wanted to be an astronaut until they told me that flowers don't bloom in space.

Chez Nous

We have the road here, the gate the key. Open the window. See the flies fly out? See the mist roll in looking for a head of hair to settle on. Listen to the silverware acting up again, banging the plates, no hands in sight, no soup in the bowl. The bottom falls out. We hang it on the ceiling. See how we will. So reel me in, take me to a matinée, pin the donkey on my tail, and low down in the backseat. Now it's spring and the blue sweet peas open the provisional morning.

When your mama can't do for you your baby must. When your baby's gone you better go downtown. They said, just shut up, rehang the doors and enter from the other side. But not me I cried, as I painted it on lash by lash. They yelled, call a plumber to untangle Slinky. Fix the pipes, raise the stakes, hire an understudy!

I took the gate off the hinge, I took the hinge off the beam and pawned it. But here on the moats of the real estate, I'm rich, on paper. All the assumptions called to the kitchen, spanked, sent to bed without any dinner. Cooked too early, I was the oldest child, I am the youngest, I ask the same Four Questions every night.

We're soft and we leak. But this is where the stalk snaps, this is where the tips touch. The filly's gone against the odds. Ma was afraid we'd "get ideas." Should I clip the coupons and move to Rio? Miss my life making something out of nothing? I just wanted a lake, I just wanted an intelligent chocolate cake. I got a Gag Order! Was it something you ate? No, it was something I read, on the memory bank, in the late afternoon, while the lingering aroma comforted the unemployed saucier in the condemned restaurant below me.

There Is a Bonelessness About

Dreams of itself. Wakes from its short nap. Yawns. Stretches its limp fleshiness. Says it could have muscles if only its childhood had been. For exercise, jumps on the couch singing *me me me*. Looks for mention of its name in the papers. If not mentioned, flails, tap dances rabidly in the elevator, pausing only to bite the other passengers. At dinner parties, insists on the head of the table. Kicks those guests who do not have its name on the tips of their tongues. Secures handmaidens, demands that each time the caretaker go to town he mention his master. Insists that all random images be attributed to it. Further demands its name appear larger than all images of its making. When brought tulips, wants a chocolate mousse (the shavings must curl just so). When sneezing, stands in front of the neighbor's refrigerator drinking directly from the mouth of a quart bottle of grape juice. Charms with a tear, detains amateur comedians on their way to an orphanage at XMAS. Bleeds venom when the caretaker lives variously and has other plans. Has toes that stick out into the aisles of crowded airplanes. Pretends to drive trains of expectations off the bridge every morning only to scuba dive into the bay each night.

Unfinished Business

Pull my string, the sun's going down. Too aggressive. Love smelled to him like stale cigarettes. Too demure. Oysters are cultivated in shallow beds. Fear of the known.

The reason, he wrote, we stopped talking, I remember, you were too smart. Strain the juice. He wants it clear and pure. Throw out the juice with the pulp. He is always planning these parties and disinviting the guests.

Thank you dear cow for the cheesecake. The field of play has been mowed. Wild life reserve, they roll up their windows. You look so innocent, he said, when you're all kissed up. Keep it light. No salt, no stinky cheese, no coconut. Raw cookie batter, you got an oven for a stomach?

I'm blue like water in dense layers. He's looking for the perfect croissant. Let's fly to Death Valley and watch the moon on the blooms. In the morning we can hike to the nearest ghost town and telegram grandma: Not dead anymore.

If only I couldn't see where ends meet. On the landscape of the beginning, two flags blow in opposite directions. At dusk, I bend to kiss you with my arms folded under the sleeves of an ancient kimono.

Lime in your papaya soup. Feeder's full of seeds. And the sun comes out when the day is done.

What Leaves

With the sun behind you, your shadow is much larger than your body. The time of day is always urgent. Now is the moment to rescind the invitation. And there in the pause, some dying cells die for good, gathering a strange but tinglingly familiar zone about them. You are vaulted in beginnings. The voice drops behind the body. How you saw it as damaged fruit, sweet, done to gone in spots. The exhaustion of form. Many desires condensed into one drop. What was the sentence that spoke through the mouth, some call for entries, some chord out of time? Now you must rest. Posed on the sofa, it was always your word against a dozen other witnesses. Too much of a good thing is barely enough. Somewhere a disaster attracts a crowd, which is seduced and repelled though gloriously present. Somewhere in the collaboration you stole all your plots from life. Has the hero met the heroine? Send the current back to the powerhouse. You have done more with less but you would like someone to write home to. It was always difficult to move unless taken by surprise. The climate is generalized. You are not alone in the landscape. And now you wake quickly from the dream so as to remember it more clearly, who entered in the night, who called you to his bedside.

III. *Distance Between Two Points*

Distance Between Two Points

As if a certain postponement knew to hold off. Until the horse stops riding us. We are whipped more than once. We spring back, we canter up to the foyer, and leap toward the credenza for the plate of sweets. We would like to ask for more favor, we would like all rattlers to curl out of our way. Instead, we sip the tea with amusement, here on the mezzanine, where the elevator never stops.

They are discussing art, she is brushing her teeth, he has a toothpick in his mouth, she has a paintbrush in her left breast pocket. In the empty room, she paints curtains on the window, she paints a bed on the floor, she paints a man in the bed.

A theory helps dissolve the problem of the day. One arm of the cactus broken by the weight of its own spine. Your first thought immediately followed by your second thought squeezed off by doubt, which you confuse with reason. If you cut your hair, I just want you to know, I might not be your friend, anymore.

Across the street, the block widens. How are things going, with your new, uh, man? Fine, just fine. Why does Amour of *Psyche and L'Amour* have wings? If you hang around birds long enough, you'll catch their habits. She did not like his flutter. She did not, admittedly, enjoy his purse.

Life on a ledge resting on a seam. The quick change of mood characteristic of horses. Complaints about the bad service on their last flight to Fiji. His three golden retrievers: here Latvia, here Lithuania, here Estonia. Her search for unique: something no one else spots at the flea market. I'm not the panting dog you knew me as.

The chips shrink. The Christmas lights short circuit. Blood on the ceiling. On the other side of the fist. The body steps out of this work. Beyond my means, beyond yours, not beyond ours. What about sudden murder by syntax. Further your mercy. Disambiguate. Rewire. Reverb. Retreat. Repeat. Recoil. Drop it.

These silences, like interruptions. You will be fed ideas from now on, from the menu overhead, you can eat what you think. Just as you are about to introduce them to one another, you forget their names. Then, the telephone number of your oldest friend. Then, how to spell the simplest words. You go back to the bank. They say your credit is poor, you were living on faith.

Better yourself. Progress is an abandoned mind. So you could go deep. As we evolve, do they. Certain behaviors drop away, except fingerprints, voiceprints, footsteps, ambition. When we are first loved, we sweeten up. Then begins the interrogation.

Suddenly I noticed a lack of growth. The fingernails remained the same length they were the month before and the hair coiled in on itself without additional weight. The mind made no new decisions and no attempt to coin new phrases. No new symptoms occurred.

Before the flood, I crave chocolate chips, which my mother craved when I was in her stomach. I am thankful that my prenatal life did not include sea cucumbers, cracker jacks, snails with structurally unsound shells.

You loiter among the lost fountains. The rain so complex, so speckled, so unwet. You were taught to believe, you were taught to turn to the music for all important correspondence. Was this tiger cage your experience of Tasmania? No wonder you imagine devils at every corner of the small room you sleep in.

It doesn't go anywhere. I'm going to get her he said over and over or she's going to get me. I tell him what I want to hear. He says, if you expect music from these well-appointed chambers, you will have to bring your own banjo. All I had was available light, so I painted the same portrait over and over on the same canvas until the oil cracked and the light came through to get me.

In order to find it, you strike lightly, veer to the right, flip over,
and bounce back across the road.

They say that birds are blind to the color blue. But a man who could burst into tears over a lost friendship was also looking for the music, though he might reach the fountain much later. And I applaud your coming in like that, with a tiny silk flag in your lapel.

It began badly when we sat down to a long dinner with the two hypnotists. Then we made the long drive home, with his long silence, as usual, interrupting me. I had no endurance for entertainment. I didn't like the young brides married to their work, either.

Don't give me those chocolate pudding eyes. You make the
same gorgeous mistakes as anyone else, you blow the password
out, you press escape.

Out of one fender grows another. Pretty soon. He had a habit of finishing her sentences, pretty soon he would disappear. The baby hangs on her mother in utter bliss, the last time this is possible. The growth of teeth breaks the tie. Sooner or later. He took the engine out, he took the hood off, he filled the cavity with a vegetable garden. After the accident.

Long ago Persian sailors beat the sea with whips, before setting
sail, to banish the devils and tell the waters not to act up while
the boats were out.

IV. Reflexive

Season Ticket

In the circle of your intentions certain spars
Remain that perpetuate the enchantment of self with self
                                        —John Ashbery

The experience that eludes you intrigues you more
than the one you're currently having. It's just
over your shoulder. Pain is the least interesting
part. They deaden the vein and draw the blood.
Pints quarts gallons graham crackers and then a
glass of Tang. They replace all of it,
for a while you are out of circulation.
Now you are strong enough to pinch hit for yourself.

For this you held yourself in.
For this you have lowered the bucket
into the well and drawn the luckiest penny.
Your pens are also full of ink.
Your sink full of dishes. The chopsticks on the table.
And the dinner bell rings.

Never mind the sacrifice of lilacs in California.
For two minutes in late summer
before your skin turns the velvety petals brown
you may bobby pin a gardenia
behind your left ear and everyone
will ask you to cater their lawn parties
and evening barbecues with avatars
of your presence.

At times the big world seems to narrow
into the little self then explodes

and the shrapnel hits your best friends
who only want to hold your hand along the way.
Did you want to stay a professional child indefinitely?
Intention hails the uncommitted virtuoso, you do
know what you want, don't you? And if you don't
you'd better have the final say silk screened onto
your gold lamé tee shirt.

What triggers declivity is so confounding
you can only proceed to eat asparagus
and pee out the impurities of bad weather
inside your spring cranium. New day
and isn't it blue-green? Is there no place
safe from the self, one narcissist asks another,
yes, the self as it indefatigably keeps company
with its own low life, bopping from
one sleazy foreign hotel to the next,
with no time to learn the future
of its own currency.
Be grateful that your friends are so interesting
that exotic mushrooms grow in the back seats
of their leaky convertibles.

You can write anywhere
and you will always say what you must say since
your name is the same, isn't it?
Have you done separating the him from the her?
A new hybrid of tangerines
is not still called mandarin oranges.

Forget that love lies in botanical ruin.
A life could change in a day
if the couriers bring new information and day two

could find you in Paris dangling your toes on the Seine
instead of chaining your pinkies to a typewriter in Dubuque
hacking out that cash crop. Oh just
a little truck garden please, and don't forget to plant
the heavenly blue morning glories reaching toward
a vacant but highly perfumed heaven. Hope springs
because the genes contain all possible geysers
and it is up to you to crack the safe
at 3 A.M. and conduct the dawn from
your highly promising podium in
the most dangerous orchestra pit. The pianos are breathing
heavily. Nijinsky awaits the tap of your baton.
Anna Pavlova rises like a phoenix
instead of a swan especially in your honor
tonight.

Dilated Narrative I

Run down stairs. The end of "downward mobility." On the
Avenue, the children in designer fashions. At the Oscar party.
In the oversized house full of grandfather clocks. Not one runs.
Answer my ad. He was dead for years, for years she answered
his mail, carefully indenting the margins the same way he had.
Banked memory. Long legs and the high cost of walking. The
crazy guy on the corner never finishes his sentences

Side street. So many skies against the turrets. Through the bay
window, petals scattered in the cobweb below the vase. The
man in the wheelchair staring at the woman in the wheelchair
moving up the hill in the rain. I decided not to get the dog
because its mouth was too small to fetch the paper. If you think
of snails as pets. He likes to put them on his chest

The cat walking across the keyboard. After a long pause. I feel as
though I'm. Your life as a percussionist. As a drum. Play ball.
Pick up sticks. Steal me home. When you don't finish dinner
does your mother say, think of people starving in, a) China,
b) India, c) Cambodia, d)

The clock you used to keep ten minutes fast catches up, now it's
precisely on time, but you are still translating the King's X. Are
you the type who says, a) it's almost 8:30, b) it's 8:24, c) it's
half past, d)

I like to fix every leak. I like to keep the cows separate from the
horses. I like a clean pig pen. I'd like a bowl of crimson clover,
hold the

Beautify the computers. A spray of pink freesias in a white saki bottle above the grey terminal. Silk teabags. Enter in an open kimono, brush against the doorframe with a message: the lost arms of Venus are calling. Tender digitals

Each day a postcard arrives. A series of cloud formations covering the same spot of sky, except the one today includes a tiny plane trapped above the vapors. Have you seen any good

I warn you. They will outgrow the space you've given them. You may have to. I will

Dilated Narrative II

I sent her a picture of the whitest sands in the world. My project was to get everybody what they wanted. Invite the camel into the tent? What better way to spend your time than surprise. We have not yet begun to confuse ourselves with someone else. Outside a loaf of bread kept upping its ante, inside the waiter swept the crumbs clean. You do that with a fork? The moon will never define the sky in this light again.

I was looking for the menu, so I gave him my profile. I like the single calendula stuck in the soda bottle on the newly veneered table, I like her scuffed loafers, his glass of hot milk, the avenue bum reading the financial pages of the morning paper.

Your bath is running, you slip back into bed, the blender is running, in your dream the room is flooded as high as the covers, you open the back door and the world is flooded up to the porch, you like to swim. A man in a stall in a car wash hosing down a St. Bernard.

Spring gives me confidence that it will not hurt me more than it has to. In the rain, at the table, I watch the birds feed with their tiny dinosaur movements, design changes in bone structure. All that work and still too short. I could not prevent the white tulip from falling over and the red one from still standing.

I declare illegal: blank stares, trailer parks, defense budgets, words on clothing. All previous self-abuse now subject to forgiveness.

I used to work here, so I consider it mine, especially that young girl reading a book on a bench beside the two Balthus prints of young girls. Then they would all stroll down the street twirling open umbrellas.

Moving across the court in the same way, over and over, fumbling every pass, until I back up, the ball socks me in the face, I fall down, I skin my knee, I get up, I move to the left, I catch the ball, I shoot a basket, my team scores.

Sweet accomplishment, the beauty of a freshly pressed blouse, on a hanger, by the open window, in the early spring breeze.

She kissed me with her bright pink lipstick, then she wiped the print off my cheek with a crumpled kleenex. Her mother before her used hankies. You had to seduce her. She said no to salami the way some respond to a lurid overture.

Geometry recapitulates the heavens, all sacrifice replaced by tenderness, permission to be late for work on account of day-dreaming.

The levee is dark along the delta, from above, the mansions separate the orchards like small markers in a victory garden. In the beginning, all embraces define themselves, all talk between our eyes refers only to itself.

You remark on the similarity of cotyledons, I have no pets but these animal silhouettes against the sky.

Backhand

She doesn't like to run because her legs are too thick. He can get way down deep in women and never touch his own bottom. She feeds everyone but only snacks. He indulges himself but the relatives think he's stingy. Her generous brother abuses his girlfriend. He rarely speaks but runs the show. Under the bleachers, the boardwalk, the woman in the tight jeans says sex is an invasion of privacy. The other one, over there, in the piazza, with a locket hanging into her cleavage, fucks like crazy. All she wants is devotion. Now the men begin to worship the women of antiquity, ignoring the accomplishments of their own wives. The landscape of his mind appears heroic but it is full of elegant infidelities. Vastness deceives the singular eye, in your wide circle of friends, no one knows you. What I know about some people I keep to myself in order to continue knowing them. Oh for something that is only itself. Within an undefined space, definition emerges as what is not there. She seems intelligent, but she is compensating. How he got what he wanted, then flicked the rest of her like an ash. How she let him. Because he was burned in the dreams, because he used sleep, she used him as information. Go ahead, tear it out, break it in the same place it has always broken. The place that never stops crying, the watercress that grows along the stream, the snakes that

Leave them while they're still clapping. Go to bed before you re-coup your resistance to dreaming. Act like the trouble they've all been waiting for. (He was the boy most likely to fail, but he succeeded) (She had everything going for her, except herself) Never close out your account at Impossible Savings & Loan. Deny the skilled torturers their most loyal subject. (Every night, she wants it every night!) Excessive loyalty to your own ideas is treason to others. (He weighs 120 pounds and has 8 blankets on his bed) She is unable to participate in the pleasures of the rich or the satisfactions of the normal. (That lady beats her cats for "going to the bathroom" in the swiss chard) Somewhere the plasma physicist begins a letter to his mother: Dear Mommy. On rare occasions, when beautiful women are alone, they eat lima beans. And brussels sprouts. And liver for breakfast. (They cry to themselves and hair grows around their nipples) Are you surprised? I reveal these secrets because I hate secrets but love mystery. Have mercy for the beautiful, the rich, the poor, the crippled, the mysterious. They are like you.

Assignment

they need dreams and action, one after the other.
　　　　　　　　　　　　　—Flaubert

Face it before about-faces. Please, don't be stingy with your memories. Revive one hour of comfort, now an episode of bliss. Ignore the construction, empty the bowl, deconstruct nostalgia. Never wait empty-handed. If your memory fails, do not confuse it with imagination, encourage amnesia so complete that even the taste of mustard seems new and strange. Listen to the plums thump as they hit the lawn in California early June. Break and enter your camouflage, ask for help but not on your knees in the jungle. Do not participate in a stranger's momentary disloyalty. Try not to throw out what you can't use, draw a circle around it or give it away. Actively endure the discomfort of silence. No one asked for you and they're not about to follow you. You will be protected by the podium but you will stand completely naked. Often clothes matter. This work is akin to racing fast cars very close to the ground then smoking a pipe in the study after dinner. The sunset has a famous reputation, leave it alone or make sure you understand the sunrise. If a small bird pecks at your window repeatedly, do not assume it wants in as it is probably enamored of its own reflection. You will have new dreams, they will ring familiar. You can start midway or go backwards or both, the narrative translates as miracle. Continue the perpetual assignments, the faculty is dead except us.

Reflexive

Eat, says the hunger.
—John Ashbery

The eruption creates its own weather. At the door she would whine, low and curdling, which would serve as a knock. Every silver lining has its own lining. These tremors encapsule a tiny hold in the lower Patagonian latitudes through which it is quite possible to crawl to safety. It was a temporary crucifixion, meaning, we always rise again. Days after the bouquet is delivered to the wrong apartment, the occupant redelivers it. You couldn't see it coming but you could tell it was leaving. The man refused to visit his wife after she miscarried a potential heir. You don't suppose the physics will ever get to the bottom of it. He suffered from metanoia, he thought he was after everything. As she read the word *mysterious,* a folding chair collapsed and the sitter was thrown onto the podium. From there the occasion began. During a depression, we are incurably flirtatious on paper as if it were money. The dotted lines he drew on her ribcage narrated exactly what he would take from her. Among the available landscapes, this one will later be seen as your life. We are inclined toward a constant leaning in the direction of the fall. He hated metaphor, he took all matter into his own hands. She refused to give in to sleep, she did not like to wait, she delighted in spoiling her appetite. A question often shifts the scenery. He would never say what he wanted, only what he would settle for. Months later, the disaster reached us in the form of brilliant sunsets. The liberal candidate loved people, he shook 42 hands every 60 seconds. No advance method, only certain forms of reconnaissance. There was widespread fear of women who battled the sentimental. After the volcano exploded, a plane flew over Spirit Lake and reported it gone. The South Vietnamese orphans, called the Dust of Life, have tattoos on the backs of their hands which say, "the ones who love me cannot find me."

Every Space Explored Yields Beauty

When he tried to leave, he noticed their hairs stuck to the cobweb on the chandelier. On the bus, sleep often begins with a jerk, like the starting of a train. Maybe maybe maybe has infinite meaning. In this Chinese restaurant, the cookies are wrapped around one fortune and one misfortune. She wanted to go for a swim, so he channeled the lagoon and built her a lake. Since I had no sugar, I was forced to tell the Appaloosa a story in which horses ruled the world. You will be paid for exactly twenty-five minutes of lunch, so don't eat the rigatoni too fast. He joined the Navy because the map of the heavens kept falling off the wall above his bed. The light through the trees of the orchard reaches us as juice. They know one another so well that she absently picks at his cuticles. If I follow your gaze, our eyes seem to cast two shadows on the same object. Daddy says people who believe in miracles are weaklings, Mommy says Daddy cries when he dreams.

Reduced Cahoots

to J. E. Jouris

During a loud thunderstorm, the woman woke only when her baby cried. We picnic on a small island that sways with every wave. Long after they parted, they would emerge from separate houses at precisely the same time. What salmon know of pink. She developed a rash on the soft underside of her writing arm. Often he would gaze at the ceiling while she lay on her stomach. The results begin the moment you do. Fifteen years after he was killed by a dune buggy, the city fathers outlawed moving vehicles on the island. Leonardo wrote backwards to frustrate his nosy housekeeper. You finally realize that being that way is what makes you that way. He plays the strings of the piano instead of the keys. She wakes every hour murmuring, are we there yet. From his training in anatomy, he shakes hands and sees only the bones. In daylight, before a rain, the morning glory closes its flower. You're beautiful, you're intelligent, we want you to be happy. The woman fell in love with the son of the doctor who delivered her. A local derelict threw iodine on a photograph of the famous artist who said anybody can do anything.

ABC's

Steal me an A before you steal home. You will receive this timeless message long after it has been introduced by the shy physical presence of the bearer. The slow mail in these parts, especially between adjoining sexes. Curiously isolated dialects. Few cognates. Intelligent lullabies, never enough sleep, and the exchange of dreamed up creation myths which make us who we are. The future of a tight squeeze. What to take on a dive. Enter the modern heroine: no equivalent in antiquity, on her way to replacing the good old boy. Bud of the blueprint. Up all night inventing systems for the retrieval of softness in our rapidly hardening world. New at the art of breathing under and over. Who says that red deep is farther than the great white. And blue is the hottest flame and the largest value above us. *The key is in the sunlight at the window*. The coast is lined with everything you thought flew away, the punks are relatively bedded down for the night, and now crack the safe and reach for all you thought was missing. The long restlessness before this which prepared us for the weight of our invisible provisions. Those whose fingers have eyes, those out of love with the symptoms, will wear the letter A embroidered on their overalls, A for the beginning of the American alphabet, A for the lost arms of Venus, A for the first time, once again, always, and never before.

650 copies of *Back to Forth* printed
February 1982, of which 10 copies
are numbered in roman numerals I–X
and signed by the author.

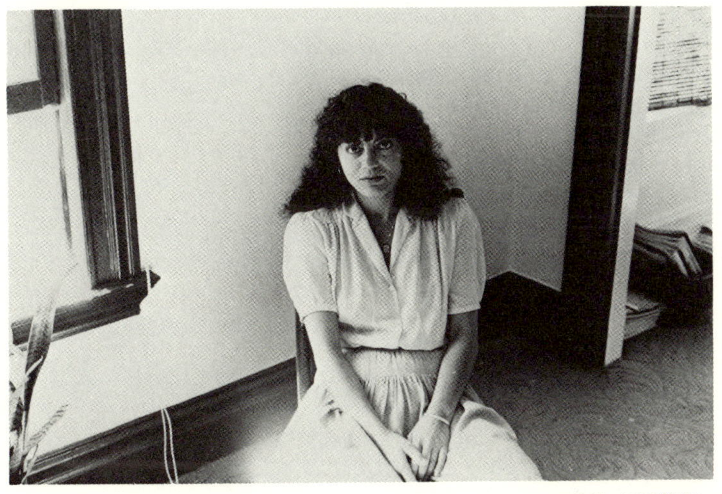

J.E. JOURIS

Gloria Frym was born in New York in 1947. She grew up in Los Angeles, lived in New Mexico for many years, and traveled in South America. Her previous books include *Impossible Affection* (Christopher's Books, 1979) and *Second Stories* (Chronicle Books, 1979). She lives in Berkeley.

THE FIGURES

Rae Armantrout *Extremities* $2.50
Paul Auster *Wall Writing* $3.00
David Benedetti *Nictitating Membrane* $3.00
Steve Benson *As Is* $3.50
Alan Bernheimer *Cafe Isotope* $3.00
John Brandi *Diary from a Journey to the Middle of the World* $4.00
Summer Brenner *From the Heart to the Center* $3.00
Summer Brenner *The Soft Room* $3.00 o.p.
David Bromige *My Poetry* $4.00
Laura Chester *My Pleasure* $3.00
Laura Chester *Watermark* $4.00
Tom Clark *Baseball* $6.50
Michael Davidson *The Prose of Fact* $5.00
Christopher Dewdney *Spring Trances in the Control Emerald Night* $2.50
Johanna Drucker *Italy* $3.50
Barbara Einzig *Disappearing Work* $4.00
Kathleen Fraser *Each Next* $3.00
Gloria Frym *Back to Forth* $4.00
Merrill Gilfillan *River Through Rivertown* $4.00
Artie Gold & Geoff Young *Mixed Doubles* $5.00
Lyn Hejinian *Writing is an Aid to Memory* $3.00
Bob Perelman *7 Works* $3.50
Tom Raworth *Ace* $2.00
Tom Raworth *Writing* $6.00
Stan Rice *Some Lamb* $4.00
Kit Robinson *Down and Back* $3.00
Stephen Rodefer *The Bell Clerk's Tears Keep Flowing* $3.00
James Schuyler *Early in '71* $2.00
Ron Silliman *Tjanting* $6.00
Julia Vose *Moved Out on the Inside* $4.00
Guy Williams *Selected Works 1976-1982* With an Essay
     by Gus Blaisdell $10.00
Geoffrey Young *Subject to Fits* $5.00